12/08

Energy for the Future

by Helen Orme

Consultant: Terry Jennings, Ph.D.
Educational Consultant

BEARPORT
PUBLISHING

New York, New York

Credits

Cover and Title Page, © ollirg/Shutterstock; Credit Page, © Otmar Smit/Shutterstock; 4, © Yvan/Shutterstock; 4–5, © digitalife/Shutterstock; 6, © amygdala imagery/Shutterstock; 6–7, © Bryan & Cherry Alexander Photography/Alamy; 8–9, © Otmar Smit/Shutterstock; 9, © Andreas Gradin/Shutterstock; 10, © Shutterstock; 10–11, © Mario Savoia/Shutterstock; 12–13, © Kamil Sobócki/Shutterstock; 14, Courtesy of NASA; 14–15, © Iain Frazer/Shutterstock; 16–17, © Roca/Shutterstock; 17, © Ria Novosti/Science Photo Library; 18–19, © Mark Smith/Shutterstock; 19, © Hywit Dimyadi/Shutterstock; 20, © Michael Shake/Shutterstock; 20–21, © Mehau Kulyk/Science Photo Library; 22, © Josep M Peñalver Rufas/Shutterstock; 22–23, © Margaud/Shutterstock; 24, © Les Scholz/Shutterstock; 25, © fStop/Alamy; 27T, © Prof. David Hall/Science Photo Library; 27B, © Science Photo Library; 28, © Adisa/Shutterstock; 29T, © Shutterstock; 29C, © Philip Lange/Shutterstock; 29B, © chiara levi/iStockphoto; 30, © Kenneth V. Pilon/Shutterstock.

Every effort has been made to trace the copyright holders, and we apologize in advance for any unintentional omissions. We would be pleased to insert the appropriate acknowledgments in any subsequent edition of this publication.

The Earth in Danger series is printed on recycled paper.

Library of Congress Cataloging-in-Publication Data

Orme, Helen.
  Energy for the future / by Helen Orme.
    p. cm. — (Earth in danger)
  Includes index.
  ISBN-13: 978-1-59716-727-7 (lib. bdg.)
  ISBN-10: 1-59716-727-4 (lib. bdg.)
  1. Renewable energy sources—Juvenile literature. 2. Power resources—Environmental aspects—Juvenile literature. 3. Energy development—Environmental aspects—Juvenile literature. I. Title.

  TJ808.2.O76 2009
  621.042—dc22
                      2008021611

Contents

The Energy Problem

People can't live without **energy**. They need it as a source of power to heat and light homes and businesses. They also need it to power many things they use each day, such as computers, cars, and TVs.

People require a lot of energy to survive. Unfortunately, there is a limited supply of many **fuels** such as oil. Also, the huge amount of fuel that people use creates **pollution**, which is harmful to the **environment**. Scientists are working to find new energy sources that will not run out and will be safer for the planet.

An oil rig

Most of the energy used in homes is for lighting and for running appliances, such as refrigerators, dishwashers, and air conditioners.

Nonrenewable Energy Sources

There are different types of energy sources. Some will last forever and others will, in time, run out. The energy sources that people use most—oil, gas, and coal—will eventually be completely used up. That's why they're called nonrenewable.

Not only will these energy sources not last forever, they're also bad for the environment. Oil, gas, and coal are **fossil fuels**. When they're burned, they give off **greenhouse gases**, such as carbon dioxide, that pollute the environment. Too much carbon dioxide in the atmosphere may cause Earth to warm up. If the planet warms up too much, many plants and animals that are used to living in cooler climates may not survive.

A coal-burning plant

Global warming is an increase in the average temperature of the air and water on Earth. Some scientists believe that if the **climate** changes too quickly, plants, animals, and people won't be able to adapt.

As temperatures rise at the North Pole, there is less and less ice for polar bears to hunt on.

Renewable Energy Sources

Sources of energy that won't run out are called renewable. The renewable energy source that people use most is the sun.

Other sources of renewable energy are wind, the movement of ocean waves and **tides**, the force of water rushing down hills and mountains, and the burning of wood. If scientists can find ways to use these sources more often, then people won't be in danger of running out of energy and causing major damage to the planet.

When wood is burned, it releases less carbon dioxide into the atmosphere than fossil fuels. So burning wood is a good way to produce energy that is less harmful to the environment.

The solar panels on this house's roof use the sun's energy to heat water and air.

Clean Energy

Clean energy is a way to provide power without harming the environment. This type of energy produces little or no polluting gases, such as carbon dioxide.

How can people use clean energy more often? People can do this by using renewable sources of energy for power—such as the wind, waves, tides, and the sun—instead of harmful fossil fuels.

The force of river water pouring through a **dam** is used to make electricity. However, there's a downside to this process. Building large dams can harm the **habitats** of thousands of plants and animals.

A dam

Mirror solar panels provide clean energy with help from the sun.

Wind and Wave Power

More and more people are using wind to provide clean energy. When wind turns the blades of a wind **turbine**, the blades spin a **generator** that produces electricity.

There are, however, a few problems with wind power. The turbines can produce power only when the wind blows. They're also huge so they take up a lot of land, often forcing wildlife from their homes. However, scientists have built some wind turbines in bodies of water, to avoid harming the habitats of plants and animals on land.

Waves and tides are also good sources of clean energy. People are only now figuring out how to turn their constant motion into power. One method being tried is to use the sea's movements to turn turbines, just as the wind turns the blades of wind turbines.

The largest wind turbine in the world is in Hawaii. It stands 20 stories high. Each of its blades is longer than a football field.

Wind turbines in the ocean

13

Solar Power

The sun is another important source of clean energy. People are using **solar panels** to turn sunlight into power.

Solar panels are used to trap the power of the sun's rays to make electricity. These panels are made up of many **solar cells**. The cells convert, or change, energy from sunlight into electrical power. This is a great way to get clean energy. Though solar panels don't work at night, the energy they collect can be stored in batteries.

In the future, it may be possible to put big solar panels into space and send the power down to Earth. The best thing about this plan is that in space the sun always shines! So power could be generated around the clock.

This building in France generates electricity using the rays of the sun.

Nuclear Power

Nuclear energy is another power source that doesn't give off carbon dioxide or other harmful gases. It's made using substances such as **uranium**.

Though nuclear energy doesn't produce harmful gases, there are some problems with it. Nuclear power stations are expensive to build and run. They also produce dangerous wastes that can make living things sick or even kill them. The wastes stay dangerous for thousands of years and must be buried in leak-proof containers deep underground. Scientists are working on new, safer types of nuclear power that may solve some of these problems.

The cooling towers of a nuclear power plant

Uranium is found deep underground and needs to be **mined**. There may not be enough uranium in the world to keep nuclear stations working in the future.

17

Cleaning Up Coal

Coal is a fossil fuel that has been used for a long time. It takes thousands of years for it to form underground.

Today, coal is one of our major sources of energy. Supplies of it are expected to last for hundreds of years. However, since it takes a long time for new coal to form, it's considered a nonrenewable energy source. Burning coal also releases more polluting gases than any other fossil fuel.

Coal can be used in ways that reduce its harm to the environment. For example, it can be sprayed with special chemicals that help it burn cleaner. The gases that are given off by burning coal can also be filtered before being released into the air. Or the polluting gases can be stored in containers that can be buried in the ground or at sea.

Some scientists believe that the methods used to clean coal may actually harm the environment.

A coal power plant

Electric Cars

Another one of the world's major sources of energy is oil. It's used to create fuel for cars, buses, and trucks. However, people need to cut back on its use because oil supplies will not last forever. Burning oil also creates lots of pollution.

One way to use less oil is for people to start driving electric cars. These vehicles don't produce harmful gases. If everyone drove one, cities would be much cleaner. When the electricity for the cars' batteries is produced at power stations that burn fossil fuels, however, then the cars may not reduce pollution very much.

Hybrid cars are powered by both oil and electricity. A hybrid car can make and store electricity while it runs on fuel. Then, when it stops, brakes, or goes downhill, it can switch to electric power and save fuel.

An electric car recharging

The Best Renewable Energy Source

One of the most promising renewable energy sources is **biomass**. Corn, trees, and sugarcane as well as sawdust, grass clippings, and peanut shells are all biomass fuels. **Methane** is another biomass fuel. It's a gas released from animal droppings and **decaying** plants. Burning these fuels doesn't put as much carbon dioxide into the air as fossil fuels.

Many scientists feel that biomass is one of the best energy sources for the future. Plants are always growing and dying, and animals are always producing waste. So there will always be a good supply of this fuel. Today, 3 percent of all the energy made in the United States comes from biomass.

Sugarcane

A field of corn

Burning wood releases carbon dioxide into the atmosphere. Trees, however, take carbon dioxide out of the atmosphere and use it to make their own food. So to help reduce pollution, it's very important to keep planting trees.

Saving Energy

The best way to save energy and help the environment is to use less power. Here are some ways people can start saving energy today.

- On cold days, wear layers of clothes inside so the heat can be kept on low.

- On warm days, open windows and use fans rather than turning on the air conditioner.

- After washing clothes, hang them up to dry rather than using a dryer.

- Close curtains and blinds at night to keep the heat in.

- Shut off all the lights before leaving a room.

- Turn off TVs and computers when not in use.

- Use only low-energy lightbulbs.

Hanging clothes out to dry saves lots of the energy that dryers, which run on gas or electricity, use.

Cars, Trucks, and Greenhouse Gases

People everywhere drive cars and trucks. In the United States, there are 765 cars for every 1,000 people. Why is this a problem?

- Most cars are fueled by gasoline, which is a fossil fuel. Burning fossil fuels creates huge amounts of greenhouse gases. Too many of these gases can cause dangerous changes in the planet's climate. For example, the gases may cause Earth to warm up, which can lead to the melting of polar ice. This will make it hard for the animals that live in polar regions to survive.

- There are many trucks on the road. More than a quarter of them carry food grown in other countries. If everyone ate locally grown food, the number of trucks that are needed might decrease. Fewer trucks mean that fewer greenhouse gases would be released. More than a quarter of all trucks travel back empty after delivering their goods. If they collected other goods for their return trips, then they would be more **energy-efficient**.

- One way to reduce greenhouse gases is to drive cars less often. More than half of the car trips most people make each day are less than half a mile (1 km) long! Walking, bicycle riding, and using public transportation are ways to reduce the use of cars for short trips. For longer trips, carpooling can help lower the number of cars on busy highways.

Planes vs. Trains

Throughout the world, about 81,000 planes take off each day. In 2003, 200 million people traveled by plane. By 2030, this number is expected to double to 400 million. Planes get people to places much faster than other types of transportation. However, they produce large amounts of greenhouses gases. What can people do to help this situation?

- They can use airplanes only for long-distance flights.

- For shorter trips, they can use trains and buses. These vehicles produce less carbon dioxide than planes, so they are **greener** ways to travel.

- This graph shows how much carbon dioxide is produced for every 100 passengers traveling 62 miles (100 km). As you can see, trains produce less carbon dioxide than either cars or planes. This means traveling by train is less harmful to the environment.

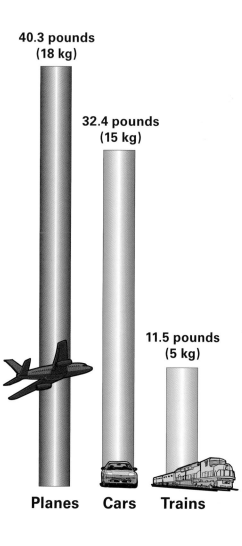

40.3 pounds (18 kg)

32.4 pounds (15 kg)

11.5 pounds (5 kg)

Planes   Cars   Trains

Biogas Plants in India

In India, burning wood is an important way to cook food. However, there isn't enough wood for everyone. So many people in India have **biogas** plants outside their homes. Biogas is produced by waste that has been decaying for a while.

- How does a biogas plant work? First, people put household waste and food scraps into a tank. Then, as the waste rots, methane gas is produced. This gas can be used as fuel for cooking, just as natural gas is used in many homes.

- On a bigger scale, the gas from biogas plants can be used as fuel for power stations that produce electricity.

A small biogas plant that could be used outside of a home

A large-scale biogas plant

Just the Facts

Power Stations

Big power stations make huge amounts of electricity. It's not enough, however, to just produce electricity.

- The electricity must be sent to where it's needed. To do this, power companies build huge towers, or pylons, like those shown below, to support cables. These structures, while necessary to carry electricity from the station into homes and businesses, are unattractive. They also disturb the habitat of hundreds of types of wildlife on land and in the air.

- Building more small power plants close to homes and businesses reduces the need to cover so much land with cables and towers. Also, small power plants can more easily produce power from renewable energy sources, such as the sun and wind, than larger plants.

- New technology allows electricity to be produced very close to the homes that use it. This reduces the need for long distance cables to deliver power.

Making Your Own Electricity

Future homes will be built to be more energy-efficient. Some may even make their own power. Here are a few ways that homes can produce electricity—maybe even enough to share with other homes.

- People can install small wind turbines near their home. If there is lots of wind the turbines will be a good source of power.

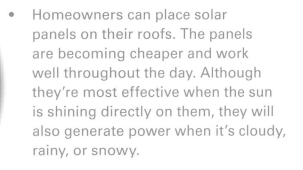

- Homeowners can place solar panels on their roofs. The panels are becoming cheaper and work well throughout the day. Although they're most effective when the sun is shining directly on them, they will also generate power when it's cloudy, rainy, or snowy.

- In the future, more homes may be equipped with fuel cells. Fuel cells contain hydrogen and oxygen. When these two gases are combined in a certain way, they create electrical power. Fuel cells will eventually replace boilers as a way to heat water.

How to Help

Here are some tips to help you become an energy saver:

- Find out who the energy champion is in your family! On a piece of paper, write down the energy-saving tips from page 24. Add columns next to the tips. Put the names of each family member at the tops of the columns. Then, anytime someone in your family follows one of the tips, place a check mark beneath his or her name in the column next to the tip. See who has the most check marks after a month.

SAVING ENERGY!				
Energy-Saving Tips	Mom	Dad	Sharon	Joe
1. On cold days, wear layers of clothes inside so the heat can be kept on low.	✓✓	✓		✓
2. On warmer days, open windows and use fans instead of air conditioners.			✓	
3. Hang up clothes to dry.	✓✓		✓	✓
4. Close curtains and blinds at night to keep in heat.				
5. Shut off the lights when leaving a room.	✓	✓		✓
6. Turn off TVs and computers when not in use.		✓	✓	✓✓
7. Use only low-energy lightbulbs.		✓		

- Instead of taking the bus or having your parents drive you, start a "walk to school" or "ride your bike to school" week with all the kids in your neighborhood. You never know—you might enjoy it so much that you will want to do it all the time!

Learn More Online

To learn more about future energy, visit
www.bearportpublishing.com/EarthinDanger

Glossary

biogas (BYE-oh-gass) gas from decaying waste that can be used as fuel

biomass (BYE-oh-*mass*) living and recently dead plant and animal material that can be used as fuel

climate (KLYE-mit) the typical weather in an area

dam (DAM) a strong barrier that's built across a river to hold back water

decaying (di-KAY-ing) rotting

energy (EN-ur-jee) power that machines, such as air conditioners and cars, need in order to work

energy-efficient (EN-ur-jee-uh-FISH-uhnt) something that uses as little energy as possible to operate; also refers to measures taken to prevent energy loss

environment (en-VYE-ruhn-muhnt) the area where animals or plants live, and all the things, such as weather, that affect the place

fossil fuels (FOSS-uhl FYOO-uhlz) fuels such as coal, oil, and gas made from the remains of plants and animals that died millions of years ago

fuels (FYOO-uhlz) things that are burned to produce heat or power

generator (JEN-uh-*ray*-tur) a machine that produces electricity

global warming (GLOHB-uhl WORM-ing) the gradual heating up of Earth's air caused by greenhouse gases trapping heat from the sun in Earth's atmosphere

greener (GREEN-ur) good for the environment

greenhouse gases (GREEN-*houss* GASS-iz) carbon dioxide, methane, and other gases that trap warm air in the atmosphere so it cannot escape into space

habitats (HAB-uh-*tats*) places in nature where animals are found

methane (METH-ayn) an odorless and colorless gas that can be made from rotting waste and is used for energy

mined (MINDE) dug up and removed from the earth

pollution (puh-LOO-shuhn) harmful materials, such as oils, wastes, and chemicals, that damage the air, water, and land

solar cells (SOH-lur SELZ) cells that can change the energy from the sun into electrical energy

solar panels (SOH-lur PAN-uhlz) groups of solar cells that are connected to form a flat surface; they trap energy from the sun and change it into electrical energy or use it to heat water

tides (TIDEZ) movement of water toward or away from the shore of an ocean or other large body of water

turbine (TUR-bine) a machine that is turned by the wind, by flowing gas, or by moving water

uranium (yu-RAY-nee-uhm) a heavy, radioactive metal that is often used to produce nuclear energy

Index

Read More

Challoner, Jack. *Energy.* New York: DK Children (2000).

Peterson, Christine. *Alternate Energy.* Danbury, CT: Children's Press
    (2004).

Saunders, Nigel. *Nuclear Energy (Energy for the Future and Global
    Warming).* Pleasantville, NY: Gareth Stevens Publishing (2007).